Highlights™

Laugh Attack!

Animal Crackups

1,001 Beastly Riddles, Jokes, and Tongue Twisters from Highlights

Illustrated by Rich Powell

Copyright © 2015 by Highlights for Children, Inc.
All rights reserved.
For information about permission to reproduce selections from this
book, please contact permissions@highlights.com.

Published by Highlights for Children, Inc.
P.O. Box 18201
Columbus, Ohio 43218-0201
Printed in the United States of America

ISBN: 978-1-62979-426-6

First edition

Visit our website at highlightspress.com.
10 9 8 7 6 5 4 3 2 1

Design by Dolores Motichka
Production by Sue Cole
The titles are set in Aachen Std Bold.
The text is set in Bones Regular.

CONTENTS

Under the Sea-Hee-Hee

What kind of fish goes well with peanut butter?
A jellyfish.

What did the fish say to the coral reef?
 "You're my worst anemone."

What kind of gum do whales chew?
 Blubber gum.

How much did the crab pay for the sandcastle?
 A sand dollar.

A fisherman carrying a lobster met a friend on his way home. "Where are you going with that lobster under your arm?" asked his friend.

The fisherman answered, "I'm taking it home to dinner."

Just then the lobster spoke up. "I've already had my dinner. May we go to a movie instead?"

What is a shark's favorite game?
Swallow the leader.

TOURIST: Where is the best place to see a man-eating fish?
AQUARIUM GUIDE: At a seafood restaurant.

What do you call a messy crustacean?
A slobster.

What did the magician say to the fisherman?
"Pick a cod, any cod."

What has ten arms and a cowboy hat
and terrorizes the ocean?
Billy the Squid.

What is the difference between a dog and a
marine biologist?
One wags a tail and the other tags a whale.

Knock, knock.
Who's there?
Urchin.
Urchin who?
Urchin has a dimple.

What fish is always the best dressed?
The swordfish, because it always looks sharp.

What do you call a fish with no eyes?
A fsh.

4

Why do sea horses like only salt water?
Because pepper water makes them sneeze.

SETH: Why didn't the octopus want to eat his dinner?

JACKSON: Because he wasn't hungry?

SETH: No, because he didn't want to wash all of his hands!

Knock, knock.
Who's there?
Walrus.
Walrus who?
Why do you walrus ask that silly question?

Why don't fish like to play basketball?
   They're afraid of the net.

What is the saddest animal in the ocean?
  The blue whale.

Why did the dolphin cross the bay?
  To get to the other tide.

What is the most expensive fish in the world?
  A goldfish.

TARA: Did you give the goldfish fresh water
  today?
MARK: No. They didn't finish the water I gave
  them yesterday.

What's the difference between a fish
and a piano?
  You can tune a piano, but you can't tuna fish.

Where do crabs keep their dishes?
In the crabinets.

What did the lobster give to its teacher?
A crab apple.

Three clams ate a chocolate bar while two angelfish watched. After the clams finished it, one of the angelfish said, "Look at that. They ate the whole thing without offering us a bite!"

The other angelfish said, "I know. They're being shellfish."

How did the fish cross the ocean?
Very e-fish-iently.

Where do sea cows sleep at night?
In the barn-acle.

BOOKS NEVER WRITTEN

Under the Sea by Coral Reef

Squid Arms by Trent Ickals

Scuba Diving Experience by Shaw A. Fish

Giant Oysters by Michelle S. Bigg

The Bottom of the Ocean by Vera Deepe

Anatomy of a Shark by Rosa Teeth

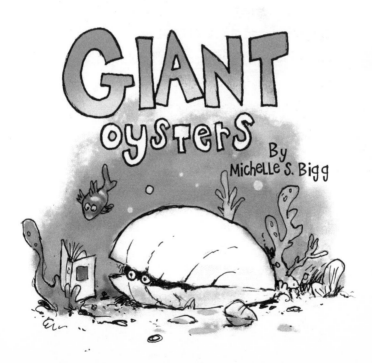

Where did the whale play his violin?
In the orca-stra.

FISHERMAN #1: I want to catch something shiny
   and expensive.
FISHERMAN #2: How about a goldfish?

Why does the ocean roar?
You would, too, if you had lobsters in your bed.

What do you call two octopuses that look alike?
I-tentacle twins.

How do fish check their weight?
With a scale.

Knock, knock.
Who's there?
Halibut.
Halibut who?
Halibut we go to the movies tonight?

What do you get when you cross a shark with a U.S. president?
Jaws Washington.

If two fish try out for choir, which one will
be chosen?

The one with better scales.

What kind of cookies do sea serpents
like to eat?

Chocolate ship.

FISH #1: Did you see that new movie last night?
FISH #2: Yes, it was fin-tastic!

What do you say to a blue whale?
"Cheer up!"

What happened to the goldfish that went bankrupt?
He's now a brass fish.

DIMITRI: What is the fastest whale in the world?
ROSS: I don't know. What is it?
DIMITRI: Moby Quick!

Why did the fish go to the library?
To find some bookworms.

What did the mother sardine say to her children when they saw a submarine for the first time?

"Don't be frightened, children—it's only a can of people."

OLIVIA: I saw a man-eating shark in the zoo aquarium.

SEAMUS: That's nothing. I saw a girl eating shrimp in the zoo restaurant.

Why couldn't Batman and Robin go fishing?

Because Robin kept eating all the worms.

Knock, knock.

Who's there?

Porpoise.

Porpoise who?

I stopped by on porpoise to see you.

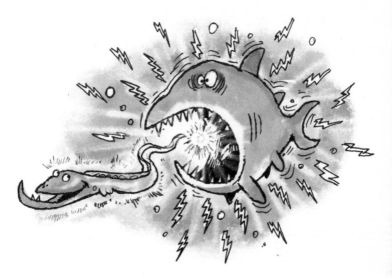

How do electric eels taste?
Absolutely shocking!

What do you get when you graduate from scuba-diving school?
A deep-loma.

Who did the boy fish go to the movies with?
His gill-friend.

What do you call a snail on a ship?
  A snailer.

What is stranger than seeing a catfish?
  Seeing a goldfish bowl.

What sharks would you find at a
construction site?
  Hammerhead sharks.

How does a fish cut through a piece of wood?
It uses a sea-saw.

What do you get when you cross a great white shark with a trumpet fish?
I don't know, but I wouldn't want to play it!

What did one tide pool say to the other tide pool?
"Show me your mussels!"

How do you make an octopus laugh?
With ten-tickles.

CORY: Have you ever seen a fish cry?
TORY: No, but I have seen a whale blubber.

What did the boy octopus say to the girl octopus?

"I wanna hold your hand, hand, hand, hand, hand, hand, hand, hand!"

Knock, knock.
Who's there?
Seaweed.
Seaweed who?
Seaweed come in if you opened the door.

A man went on a fishing trip, but at the end of the day, he had not caught a single fish. He stopped at a fish vendor on his way home.

"Hello," he said to the vendor, "I'd like to buy three fish, please. But can you throw them to me?"

The vendor replied, "Why on earth do you want me to do that?"

The man said, "So that I can tell everyone I caught three fish!"

What is a dolphin's favorite television show?
Whale of Fortune.

What fish is always asked to sign autographs?
A starfish.

Who was the most famous shark writer?
William Sharkspeare.

What do sharks say when something cool happens?

"That is jawsome!"

What do fish sing at Christmas?

Christmas corals.

What is the best way to get a fish to keep a secret?

Tell it not to tell a sole.

TONGUE TWISTERS

Orcas orchestrate organized outings.

Porpoises parading in purple pajamas.

Fish scales—shining, silvery!

Sasha shivered as she saw sharks.

Nine white narwhals whistled wildly in the water.

Baby barracudas slurp blueberries.

Selfish shellfish.

Freda feeds the fish fresh food.

Squids squirt sticky substances.

Walruses wipe windows with white wrinkled rags.

Six shiny sharks shared shortbread.

Chitters, Twitters, Squawks

What bird is always out of breath?
A puffin.

Knock, knock.
Who's there?
Toucan.
Toucan who?
Toucan play this game.

Why was the owl a great investigative
reporter?
   He was always asking, "Who? Who? Who?"

Whom do birds marry?
Their tweethearts.

What is a bird's favorite game?
Fly-and-seek.

What do you get when you cross a caterpillar
and a parrot?
A walkie-talkie.

What song do penguins sing on a birthday?
"Freeze a Jolly Good Fellow."

What sound does a hummingbird make while
she's thinking?
"Hmmm."

What do ducks wear to fancy events?
Ducksedos.

How did the bird get to the doctor's office?
He flu.

Why did the seagull fly over the sea?
*Because if he flew over the bay, he'd
be a bagel.*

What is a bird's favorite drink?
Hot coo-coo.

Knock, knock.
Who's there?
Why do owls go.
Why do owls go who?
Because that's how they talk, silly!

OZZIE: How much birdseed should I buy?

STORE CLERK: How many birds do you have?

OZZIE: None, but I want to grow some.

What do you call a crate full of ducks?
A box of quackers.

Where do penguins like to go swimming?
The South Pool.

How is a penny like a turkey sitting on a fence?
Head's on one side, tail's on the other.

JAKE: What do most birds have?
JILLIAN: Wings.
JAKE: Can you repeat that?
JILLIAN: Wing! Wing! Wing!
JAKE: Hello? Hello?

Why do penguins carry fish in their beaks?
Because they haven't got any pockets.

TALLULAH: Turkey, what are you thankful for?
TURKEY: Tofu!

What is black and white and blue all over?
A shivering penguin.

Why does a flamingo
stand on one leg?
*Because if it lifted both
legs, it would fall over!*

The ticket seller at a high-school basketball game let in the chicken, the turkey, the pheasant, and the goose, but he turned away the duck. Why?

Because five fowls and you're out.

When do ducks wake up in the morning?

At the quack of dawn.

Knock, knock.
Who's there?
Ostrich.
Ostrich who?
Ostrich my arms up to the sky.

Why do hummingbirds hum?
   Because they don't know the words.

What animal grows down?
   A duck.

How many toucans can replace a light bulb?
   Two can.

Why do birds fly south in the winter?
   It's too far to walk.

MARIELLE: I know someone who thinks he's an owl.

MIGUEL: Who?

MARIELLE: Make that two people.

KIM: How much is that bird?

CLERK: Ten dollars, ma'am.

KIM: I'll take him. Will you send me the bill?

CLERK: I'm sorry, ma'am. You'll have to take the whole bird.

How do baby birds learn how to fly?
They just wing it.

How to Catch Worms by Earl E. Bird
Australian Birds by Oz Trich
Egg Shells by Babe E. Birds
Where's My Tuxedo? by Penny Gwinn
Pink Feathers by Flo Mingo

What do you call a bird that smells bad?
A foul fowl.

What did the veterinarian give the sick bird?
Tweetment.

What was the goal of the detective duck?

To quack the case.

Knock, knock.

Who's there?

Baby owl.

Baby owl who?

Baby owl see you later or baby owl just
call you.

MEL: What kind of bank does a penguin go to?

MINNIE: I don't know. What kind?

MEL: A snowbank.

What kind of bird never goes to the barber?

A bald eagle.

How do birds fly in the rain?

They use their wing-shield wipers.

What bird can lift the most weight?
A crane.

Knock, knock.
Who's there?
Stork.
Stork who?
Better stork up on food before the storm.

What do you call a bird that stays up north
during winter?
A brrrrrd.

Why did the robin sniffle and cry on
February 29?
Because it was a weep year.

What kind of fish do penguins catch at night?
Starfish.

JAMES: What did the crow say to the robber?

THALIA: I don't know. What?

JAMES: "Stop in the name of the caw!"

Knock, knock.

Who's there?

Turkey.

Turkey who?

Turkey, open door.

What is the saddest bird?
The blue jay.

What did the duck do after the goose told him a joke?
He quacked up.

Who is a penguin's favorite aunt?
Aunt Arctica.

JENNIFER: Do you want to hear a bird joke?

RAVI: No, thanks.

JENNIFER: Well, this is "hawk"ward . . .

Knock, knock.
Who's there?
Who.
Who who?
I didn't know you spoke Owl!

Why are pigeons so good at baseball?
   Because they always know how to get home.

What is a bird's favorite food?
   A-sparrow-gus.

LINDA: What's black and white and red all over?
TAYLOR: I don't know. What?
LINDA: A sunburned penguin.

Who does a duck visit when he feels sick?
A ducktor.

How is a peacock like the number 9?
It's nothing without its tail.

What is the difference between a fly
and a bird?
A bird can fly, but a fly can't bird!

Knock, knock.
Who's there?
Wren.
Wren who?
Wren you're finished, please put it away.

What's noisier than a whooping crane?
A trumpeting swan.

What's orange and sounds like a parrot?
A carrot.

Who stole the soap from the bathtub?
   The robber ducky.

What do you get when you cross a bird, a car,
and a dog?
   A flying carpet.

What animal has fangs and webbed feet?
Count Duckula.

What is the rudest bird?
A mockingbird.

Knock, knock.
Who's there?
Owls.
Owls who?
Of course they do—everybody knows that.

A rooster sat on top of a barn. If it laid an egg, which way would it roll?
Roosters don't lay eggs!

What do you get when you cross a parrot with a woodpecker?
A bird that talks in Morse code.

JULIAN: Have you heard the story about the peacock.

MORGAN: Yes. It is a beautiful tale!

What do you call a crow that walks on a high wire?

An a-crow-bat.

What should you do if something throws a goose at you?

Duck.

What do you get when you cross a parrot and a shark?

A bird that talks your ear off.

Why did the rooster cross the road?

To prove he wasn't chicken.

ANNIE: Hello, I'd like to buy a bird.

PET STORE WORKER: Okay, what kind would you like?

ANNIE: One that goes cheep.

What is a turkey's favorite dessert?
  Cherry gobbler.

MILICA: Mom, I think I'm coming down with a cold. I've been sneezing all day!

MOM: I'll make you some chicken noodle soup. That's good for a cold.

MILICA: Not if you're a chicken!

Pheasants present pleasant presents.

Pudgy penguins picked pretty posies.

A gaggle of giddy geese.

Peacocks peep past pretty parrots.

Egrets grow greatly.

Flocks flee fall trees.

Gray geese graze in the green grass.

Swans squabble with squawking quails.

Waggish Dogs
and Comical Cats

What did the dog say to the car?
"Hey, you're in my barking spot!"

What did the cat say when he stubbed his toe?
  "Me-ow!"

BLAKE: My dog's the smartest in town. He can
  say his own name in perfect English.
ALLIE: What's his name?
BLAKE: Ruff.

Knock, knock.
Who's there?
Me.
Me who?
You sure have a funny-sounding cat.

What kind of dog can tell time?
A clocker spaniel.

What did the cat say after telling a funny joke?
"I'm just kitten right meow!"

Why do you have to be careful when it's raining cats and dogs?
So you don't step in a poodle.

What kind of dog is like a vampire?
A bloodhound.

KAREEM: Why did you name your dog Stripe? He's a Dalmatian with black spots.

ROZ: Well, my other pet is named Spot.

KAREEM: I didn't know you had another Dalmatian.

ROZ: I don't. My other pet is a zebra.

What did the boy say when his dog ran away?
"Well, doggone!"

How do you get a cat to do tricks?
Put a dog in a cat suit.

What U.S. state do cats and dogs like to visit?
Petsylvania.

What is a dog's favorite book?
Hairy Pawter and the Deathly Howls.

What do you call a dog who builds
doghouses?

   A barkitect.

Knock, knock.
Who's there?
Feline.
Feline who?
I'm feline fine, thanks.

Knock, knock.
Who's there?
Detail.
Detail who?
Detail of de cat is on de end.

Why did the dog leap for joy?
Joy was holding the cookies.

What is a cat's favorite color?
Purr-ple.

How do you know when your dog has gotten into the blue paint?

There are blueprints all over the house.

What do you call a cat that goes to the beach on Christmas?

Sandy Claws.

Two boys were arguing about whose dog was smarter.

TED: My dog can roll over and shake your hand.

FRED: I know.

TED: How?

FRED: My dog told me!

What's worse than raining cats and dogs?

Hailing taxi cabs.

Two men sat on a park bench. A dog sat between them. The first man asked, "Does your dog bite?"

"No, it doesn't," said the second man. So the first man put out his hand to pet the dog.

Chomp! The dog bit his finger.

"I thought you said your dog doesn't bite!" cried the first man.

"It doesn't," said the second man, "but that's not my dog."

CHARLIE: What's your dog's name?
CHELSEA: Ginger.
CHARLIE: Does Ginger bite?
CHELSEA: No, but Ginger snaps.

What time would it be if you saw ten dogs chasing a cat up a tree?

Ten after one.

What kind of bones do dogs not like?

Trombones.

What did the cat say when it struck out of the baseball game?

"Me-out?"

FIRST CAT: My owner won a trip to Australia.

SECOND CAT: Did he go?

FIRST CAT: Yes, five years ago. He's been trying to win a trip back ever since.

What do lazy dogs do?
They chase parked cars.

Why did the cat lie on the computer?
To keep an eye on the mouse.

Why can't Dalmatians play hide-and-seek?
They'll always be spotted.

Knock, knock.
Who's there?
Pooch.
Pooch who?
Pooch your coat on—it's cold outside.

BOOKS NEVER WRITTEN

How to Wash a Dog by Al Wet

How to Keep Your Pet Healthy by Ray B. Shot

What Dogs Do by Heidi Bones

Bathing Your Cat by Manny Scratches

Day in the Life of a Groomer by Harry Doggs

Sick Pets by Trudy Vett

What do you call a dog magician?
  A labracadabrador.

What do you say to a dog with a sore paw?
  "Heal, boy, heal!"

What did the dog say to the tree?
   "My bark is louder than yours!"

DAMIAN: My cat plays chess.
SEIKO: Your cat must be really smart!
DAMIAN: Oh, I don't know. I usually beat him two
   out of three times.

What do you call a dog that has the flu?
   A germy shepherd.

What do you spray to make a cat happy?
   Purr-fume.

What position does a dog play on the
football field?
   Rufferee.

Knock, knock.
Who's there?
Beagle.
Beagle who?
Beagle with cream cheese.

JORDAN: Do you have any dogs going cheap?
PET STORE OWNER: No, sir. All of our dogs
go "Woof."

What kind of cat likes looking at his reflection?
A meerkat (mirror cat).

What did the spy name her dog?
Snoopy.

How do cats and dogs order their things?
They use a cat-a-dog.

SAMMY: What kind of dog is that?

MIA: He's a police dog.

SAMMY: He doesn't look like a police dog.

MIA: That's because he's an undercover agent.

When is a dog's tail like a farmer's cart?
When it's a-waggin' (wagon).

Knock, knock.
Who's there?
Isabelle.
Isabelle who?
Isabelle on the cat's collar?

When is it bad luck to see a black cat?
When you're a mouse.

What kind of pet can't be found at a pet store?
A trumpet.

KATE: Did you like the story about the dog that ran two miles just to pick up a stick?
NATE: Well, I thought it was a little far-fetched.

Why don't dogs like being on boats?
Because the waters are too "ruff."

What did the cat say after she made fun of another cat?
"I'm sorry I hurt your felines. I was just kitten."

Why did the man take his dog to the railroad station?
To get him trained.

How can you find out a dog's name?
  Collar ID.

Knock, knock.
Who's there?
Meow.
Meow who?
Take meow to the ball game!

What kind of dog's favorite subject is science?
  A lab.

CAMP COUNSELOR: This is a dogwood tree.
CAMPER: How can you tell?
CAMP COUNSELOR: By its bark.

What did the police dog say to the speeder?
  "Stop in the name of the paw!"

Why did the police officer give the dog a ticket?
He was in the No Barking zone.

What do you call a cat that drank too much lemonade?
A sourpuss.

If dogs go to obedience school, where do cats go?

Kittygarten.

What is a dog's least favorite place to shop?

The flea market.

A woman walked into a pet store and asked, "Can I get a kitten for my apartment?"

"Sorry," said the store owner, "we don't do trades."

Ten cats were on a boat. One jumped off. How many were left?

None—they were all copycats.

LIAM: Does your puppy have a license?
LESLIE: No, he's not old enough to drive.

What did the dog say when he sat on sandpaper?

"Ruff!"

What is the unluckiest kind of cat to have?

A catastrophe.

Why does a mouse like the letter *S*?
  It makes a cat scat.

Knock, knock.
Who's there?
Aware.
Aware who?
"Aware, aware has my little dog gone?"

TOMMY: Why is your dog wearing glasses?
DANYA: Because contacts bother his eyes.

What dog loves to take bubble baths?
  A shampoodle.

What did the lazy cat say to the rat?
  "Catch you later."

What is it called when a cat wins a dog show?
  A cat-has-trophy!

What do you get if you cross a sheepdog with
a jellyfish?
  The collie wobbles.

HEATHER: Do you know why dogs run in circles?

LEO: No. Do you?

HEATHER: It must be because it's too hard to run in squares.

What do you get when you cross a dog with a frog?

A dog that can lick you from the other side of the road!

What kind of dog is made of concrete?
No dog is made out of concrete. I just threw in the concrete to make it hard.

How did the little Scottish dog feel when he saw a monster?
Terrier-fied.

What do cats like to eat on sunny days?
Mice-cream cones.

MADDIE: It's pouring outside. It's really raining cats and dogs!
AHMED: It's okay—as long as it doesn't reindeer.

What happened to the dog that swallowed a firefly?
He barked with de-light!

Knock, knock.
Who's there?
Champ.
Champ who?
Champoo the dog. He needs a bath!

What did the alien say to the cat?
   Take me to your litter.

What do cats eat for breakfast?
   Mice crispies.

What do you call a frozen dog?
   A pupsicle.

What do you call a pile of kittens?
   A meowntain.

TONGUE TWISTERS

Drew's dog Denny got drenched.

Katrina's cat chomped kibble.

Careless cats clawed and crawled.

The beagle brought bagels for breakfast.

Donald's dogs dug deep.

Five flying felines fled fleas.

Bugs and Slugs

What do you call an
undercover arachnid?
A spy-der.

A team of little animals and a team of big animals decided to play football. During the first half of the game, the big animals were winning. But during the second half, a centipede joined the game, and the little animals started to catch up. The centipede scored so many touchdowns that the little animals won the game. When the game was over, the chipmunk asked the centipede, "Where were you during the first half?"

"Putting my shoes on," the centipede said.

Knock, knock.
Who's there?
Termites.
Termites who?
Termite's the night we're going out.

Why did the bee go to the doctor?
   He had hives.

What did the spider do when he got a
new car?

He took it out for a spin.

What's worse than a giraffe with a sore throat?

A centipede with athlete's foot.

Why couldn't the bee talk to his friend?

He was too bee-sy.

Knock, knock.

Who's there?

Gnats.

Gnats who?

Gnats not a bit funny.

Why did the boy throw the butter out the window?

To see the butterfly.

What kind of bees are bad at football?
Fumblebees.

FIRST FIREFLY: You've gotten taller since I last saw you.
SECOND FIREFLY: I guess I'm having a glow spurt!

What do you call a really big ant?
A gi-ant.

What kind of insect can you wear?
A yellow jacket.

What is green and can jump a mile in a minute?
A grasshopper with hiccups.

Where would you put an injured insect?
In an antbulance.

What kind of bug can you throw?

A Fris-bee.

What do you call the event where spiders get married?

A webbing.

What's the difference between a flea and an elephant?

An elephant can have fleas, but a flea can't have elephants!

Knock, knock.
Who's there?
Roach.
Roach who?
I roach you a letter. Did you get it?

AMELIA: What has nine legs, twenty eyes, and pink fur?

MATT: I don't know.

AMELIA: I don't know either, but it's crawling on your shoulder!

What does a bug do after he has a cold?
He dis-insects (disinfects) his room.

PASSENGER ON PLANE: Those people down there
look like ants!
FLIGHT ATTENDANT: They are ants. We haven't
left the ground yet.

How do fleas travel from place to place?
They itch-hike.

Where do bees go when they get hurt?
To the waspital.

How do fireflies start a race?
"Ready, set, glow!"

Itchy Bugs by Amos Keeto

Spider By Your Foot by Don Scream

Speckled Fellows by Lady Buggs

Mysterious Buzzing Noises by Bea Byflower

Before the Cocoon by Kat R. Pillar

One Thousand Shoes for One Thousand Feet
   by Millie Pede

A snail was climbing up a cherry tree when a beetle spotted it. "Hey," said the beetle, "there aren't any cherries on that tree yet."

"I know," replied the snail, "but there will be by the time I get up there."

Knock, knock.
Who's there?
Spider.
Spider who?
In spider everything, I still like you.

Why wouldn't they let the stinkbug into the movies?
Because he had only one scent (cent).

What is the biggest ant in the world?
An elephant.

What happened to the two bedbugs who met
in the mattress?
   They got married in the spring.

What is the definition of a caterpillar?
   A worm in a fur coat.

Knock, knock.
Who's there?
Weevil.
Weevil who?
Weevil stay only a few minutes.

What is an insect's favorite sport?
  Cricket.

Which type of bee is hard to understand?
  A mumblebee.

What do you get when you cross a chicken and a centipede?

Enough drumsticks to feed an army.

PATIENT: I have butterflies in my stomach.

DOCTOR: Did you take an aspirin?

PATIENT: Yes, and now they're playing Ping-Pong.

What did the bee say when it returned to the hive?

"Honey, I'm home."

What do you call a party for fleas?

A flea-esta.

What do you call a fly with a damaged wing?

A walk.

CAMP COUNSELOR: How did you get that horrible swelling on your nose?

JIMMY: I bent down to smell a brose.

CAMP COUNSELOR: There's no *b* in rose.

JIMMY: There was in this one!

What kind of medicine do ants take?
   Ant-ibiotics.

Knock, knock.
Who's there?
Flea.
Flea who?
Flea blind mice.

What do you call a bug that can jump over a cup?
   A glasshopper.

What do you get when you cross a tarantula
with a rose?
I'm not sure, but I wouldn't try smelling it!

What do you call a musical insect?
A humbug.

What goes *zzub, zzub?*
    A bee flying backwards.

What does a spider do when he gets angry?
    He goes up the wall.

Why did the lady who swallowed a fly have to miss work?
    She had a stomach bug.

CUSTOMER: Waiter, there is a bee in my alphabet soup!

WAITER: Yes, sir. I'm sure there is an *A*, a *C*, and all the other letters, too.

What is smarter than a talking bird?
    A spelling bee.

What did one girl firefly say to the other girl firefly?
 "You glow, girl!"

How do you find where a mosquito has bitten you?
 Start from scratch.

What do insects learn at school?
 Mothmatics.

Two ants were running across the top of a cereal box. One stopped and said to the other, "Hey, why are we running so fast?"

"Didn't you read what it says here?" answered the other ant. "'Tear across the dotted line!'"

What are caterpillars afraid of?
   Dog-erpillars.

When did the fly fly?
   When the spider spied her.

Knock, knock.
Who's there?
Beehive.
Beehive who?
Beehive yourself or else.

FLEA #1: Well, should we go into town?
FLEA #2: Sure! Do you want to walk or take
the dog?

Who is the king of the insects?
The monarch butterfly.

What is a bumblebee's least favorite
musical note?
Bee flat.

When did the bee get married?
When he found his honey.

Why was the baby ant confused?
All of his uncles were ants.

What kind of bee trips over his own feet?
A stumblebee.

What did the spider have for lunch?
A hamburger and flies.

What did the slug say as she slid down the wall?
"My, how slime flies!"

Why don't vampires like mosquitoes?
Too much competition!

What is the strongest animal?
A snail. It carries its house on its back.

DINER: What is this fly doing in my ice cream?
WAITER: I believe it's downhill skiing, sir.

What's the difference between a coyote
and a flea?

*One howls on the prairie; the other prowls
on the hairy.*

What does a snail riding on a turtle's back say?
   "Woo-hoo!"

What do you call a cricket when he's nervous?
   A jitterbug.

What is the biggest moth in the world?
   A mammoth.

How do you know which end of a worm is
its head?

Tickle the middle and see which end laughs.

While eating dinner, a boy turns to his
father and asks, "Dad, are bugs good to eat?"

"You shouldn't ask such a gross question
over dinner," the dad says.

After dinner, the dad asks, "Now, son, what
did you want to ask me?"

"Oh, nothing," the boy says. "There was a
bug in your soup, but now it's gone."

When is a baseball player like a spider?

When he catches a fly.

Who comes to a picnic but is never invited?

Ants.

What is on the ground and also a hundred feet in the air?

A centipede on its back.

What was William Shakespeare's most famous quote about insects?

"To bee or not to bee."

How does a firefly say good-bye?

"Got to glow!"

What goes *hum-choo, hum-choo*?

A bee with a cold.

What has antlers and sucks blood?

A moose-quito.

TONGUE TWISTERS

Talented tarantulas taught tennis.

Andy asked Aunt Annie all about ants.

Swish! Three pesky mosquitoes scattered.

Spiders spin wide, webbed spirals.

Six slow snails slid silently.

Big Billy Bee buzzes by Benny Beetle.

The quick cricket wove crooked quilts.

Funnies on the Farm

Why did the farmer cross the road?
To bring back his chicken.

What is a cow's favorite painting?
Moona Lisa.

ANDY: I just bought a farm, and I can't decide
which to buy first—a tractor or a cow.
CHUCK: You'd look pretty silly riding around
on a cow.
ANDY: I'd look even sillier trying to milk a tractor.

Why did Mozart get rid of his chickens?
They kept saying, "Bach, Bach, Bach."

What does a sheep say when he meets
someone new?
"It's nice to meet ewe."

Knock, knock.
Who's there?
Cock-a-doodle.
Cock-a-doodle who?
Not cock-a-doodle who, you silly chicken,
cock-a-doodle-doo!

Why did the chicken stay home from school?
It had the people pox.

What happens when a cow doesn't shave?
He gets a moostache.

Why did the chicken cross the road, roll in the mud, then cross the road again?
It was a dirty double-crosser.

What do you call a sheep with no legs?
A cloud.

What author do hens love?
Charles Chickens.

How do you keep milk from getting sour?
You leave it in the cow.

What kind of animal would you get if you crossed a cocker spaniel, a poodle, and a rooster?
An animal that says, "Cocker-poodle-doo."

PIG: Why are you eating alphabet soup?
COW: Because if I were eating number soup,
I'd be a cow-culator!

Who is the smartest pig in the world?
Albert Einswine.

SARA: Look at that bunch of cows.

FARMER: Not bunch. Herd.

SARA: Heard what?

FARMER: Of cows.

SARA: Sure, I've heard of cows.

FARMER: No! A cow herd.

SARA: So what? I have no secrets from cows!

What is a cow's favorite musical?
The Sound of Moo-sic.

What do you
call a pig with
laryngitis?
Disgruntled.

Why does a chicken sit on her eggs?
Because she doesn't have a chair.

Knock, knock.
Who's there?
Goat.
Goat who?
Goat to the door and find out!

What has twelve tails, one horn, and squeals?
A dozen pigs in a truck.

What does a cow use to cut grass?
A lawn moo-er.

What is a pig's favorite snack?
Spighetti.

What do you call a sleeping bull?
A bulldozer.

What is a pig's favorite color?
Mahogany.

Knock, knock.
Who's there?
Lass.
Lass who?
That's what cowboys and cowgirls use to rope
    calves, isn't it?

How do pigs write top-secret messages?
With invisible oink.

Why do sheep dislike crowds?
They're very baaashful.

A woman crawled under a fence to pick some flowers in a pasture. After she had picked a few, she heard a snort. She looked up and saw a bull heading her way. She yelled to the owner of the bull, "Is that bull safe?"

The owner replied, "He is, but you aren't!"

How do you make a milkshake?
Give a cow a pogo stick.

What do you get when you cross a pig
with a tree?

A pork-u-pine.

TEACHER: Name five things that contain milk.
REILLY: Five cows.

What did the chicken's fortune cookie say?

"I wish you lots of cluck."

What do you call the story of the Three
Little Pigs?

A pig tale.

Why did the sheep have to put on a Band-Aid?

Because he was bleating.

COW: How many chicks were born to the mother hen?

ROOSTER: Take a guess.

COW: Four?

ROOSTER: You are eggs-actly right.

What do cows do on January 1?
They celebrate the "moo" year.

What do you call a pig that does karate?
A pork chop.

Knock, knock.
Who's there?
Pig.
Pig who?
Pig up your feet or you'll trip.

Why did the duck become a spy?
Because he was good at quacking codes.

Why did the sheep jump over the moon?
Because the cow was on vacation.

What do you call a cow that won't give milk?
  A milk dud.

What do you get when you play tug-of-war
with a pig?
  Pulled pork.

FARMER: I had ten cows and ten horses. They stampeded, and the horses went north.

NEIGHBOR: Where did the cows go?

FARMER: The udder way.

How does a pig get to the hospital?
In a hambulance.

What wakes up a rooster?
An alarm clock-a-doodle-doo.

What do you get when you cross a sheep and a porcupine?
An animal that can knit its own sweaters.

MATT: What would you do if a bull charged you?

AMY: I would pay him with cash.

What kind of pictures do lambs paint?

Lambscapes.

What kind of cow can drive a tractor?

A steer.

Knock, knock.
Who's there?
Candy.
Candy who?
Candy cow jump over de moon?

Why did it take the pig hours to cross
the road?

Because he was a slow-pork.

What do chickens put in their gardens?

Eggplants.

Knock, knock.
Who's there?
Cows go.
Cows go who?
No, cows go moo!

Why is it so hard to talk with a goat?
Because the goat always butts in.

What do you call a pig that sat in the sun
too long?
Bacon.

What has four legs and says, "Oom, oom"?

A cow walking backwards.

RORY: Do you have your hen-way, Joe?

JOE: What's a hen-way?

RORY: Oh, about three or four pounds.

What is a chicken's favorite musical?

Bantam of the Opera.

A man who had lived in the city all his life was visiting a farm. Pointing to a field, he asked the farmer, "Why doesn't that cow have horns? I thought cows had horns."

"Well," said the farmer, "some cows do have horns, and some cows don't. And that cow is a horse."

BOOKS NEVER WRITTEN

The World According to Pigs by Ima Hog

The Benefits of Milk by Cal C. Uhm

What to Do with Sheep Wool by Meg A. Sweater

Cute Little Piglets by Wanda Pettem

In the Pigpen by Barry Messy

Where's the Chicken? by A. Ross DaRoad

What to do with Sheep's Wool

By Meg A. Sweater

Why do cows wear bells?
Because their horns don't work.

DOG: Where do you get your hair cut?
SHEEP: At the baa-baa shop.

What do you call a pig that won the lottery?
Filthy rich.

LONNIE: Does a cow remind you of something?

JENNIE: No, but it does ring a bell.

Where do chickens like to sit on a plane?
The wing.

POLLY: Did you know that it takes three sheep
to make a sweater?

MOLLY: No—I didn't even know sheep could knit!

What did the cow say when it had nothing to
eat but a thistle?
"Thistle have to do."

Knock, knock.
Who's there?
Chicken.
Chicken who?
Better chicken the oven—something's burning.

A teacher asked her students to draw cows eating grass. One student drew a cow on the paper with no grass. The teacher asked, "Why didn't you draw any grass?"

The student replied, "The cow ate it all!"

What did the farmer put on his sick pig to cure it?

Oinkment.

What does a polite cow greet someone?

"How do you moo?"

What do you call a poem recited by a chicken?

Poultry (poetry).

How do sheep carry their homework?

In baaackpacks.

JACKIE: Why did the duck cross the road?

RANEEM: I don't know. Why?

JACKIE: To get the *Times*. Do you get it?

RANEEM: No, I get the *Journal News*!

What was the first animal in space?
   The cow that jumped over the moon.

What does cows' milk have that is good for us?
Cow-cium (calcium).

What happened when the pigpen broke?
The pig had to use a pencil.

COLIN: You should never insult a chicken.

STACEY: OK. Why not?

COLIN: It's just bad cluck!

Where does a baby cow eat?
At the calf-eteria.

How do Spanish sheep say "Merry Christmas"?
"Fleece Navidad!"

TURTLE: Which way did the cow go?

COW: I don't know. Which way?

TURTLE: The Milky Way!

What kind of machine lifts pigs?
A porklift.

Knock, knock.
Who's there?
Barbara.
Barbara who?
"Barbara black sheep, have you any wool?"

What did the farmer say to the cows at night?
   "It's pasture bedtime."

How did the chicken get off the highway?
   He took the eggs-it.

What is a sheep's favorite food?
   A chocolate baaar.

FARM HELPER: Can you tell me how long cows
   should be milked?
FARMER: They should be milked the same as
   short cows.

Where do cows go on vacation?
Moo York.

KERRY: Where does a donkey go on a field trip?

PERRY: I don't know. Where?

KERRY: To a mule-seum!

What is a cow's favorite condiment?
  Moostard.

What do goats sit on when they're watching a baseball game?

Bleat-chers.

CAMILLE: What did one cow say to the other cow on Christmas Day?

MELISSA: "Dairy Christmas!"

What do you get when you cross an angry sheep and an upset cow?

An animal that's in a baaaaaaad mooooooood.

IMANI: What do you call a baby cow?

BECKY: A calf.

IMANI: What do you call a mother cow just after she had a baby calf?

BECKY: I don't know. What?

IMANI: De-calf-inated.

CHICKEN #1: I hope our aunt gets her birthday card in time.

CHICKEN #2: Don't worry. I sent it by eggspress mail.

Why did the farmer name his pig Ink?
  Because it always ran out of the pen.

Rowdy roosters ramble around the barnyard.

Shepherds schlepping spoiled sheep.

Sweep swiftly while swine sleep.

Cheeping chicks peeped sleepily.

Greedy goats pluck grapes.

Roosters rouse resters from their roosts.

Are you sure our shaggy sheep were shorn?

One must milk many cows daily at the dairy.

Monkey Business

What is a chimpanzee's favorite flavor
of ice cream?

Mint chocolate chimp.

GORILLA KEEPER: My gorilla is sick. Do you know a good animal doctor?

ZOOKEEPER: No, I'm afraid all the doctors I know are people.

What is the first thing a monkey learns in school?

His ape, B, C's.

Why did King Kong climb the Empire State Building?

Because he couldn't fit in the elevator.

Knock, knock.

Who's there?

Gorilla.

Gorilla who?

Gorilla cheese sandwich for me, if you please.

Who was the chimp's favorite American president?

Ape-raham Lincoln.

What is a monkey's favorite dessert?

Meringue-utan.

Why do gorillas have big nostrils?

Because they have big fingers.

JULIE: What's the difference between a chimpanzee and a carton of milk?

RYAN: I don't know. What?

JULIE: Remind me not to send you to the grocery store!

Why can't you take a picture of a monkey with a hat?

Because you can't take a picture with a hat!

Why did the monkey eat so many bananas?

He liked them a bunch.

What did the orangutan say when he found out his sister had a baby?

"Well, I'll be a monkey's uncle!"

How do monkeys stay in shape?

They go to the jungle gym.

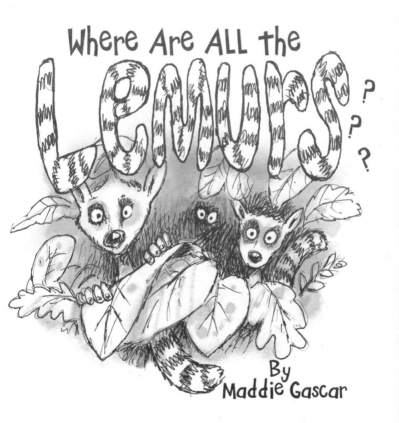

Where Are ALL the LEMURS???

By Maddie Gascar

The World of Apes by Jim Panzee

Monkey Food by Bea Nana

Where Are All the Lemurs? by Maddie Gascar

Orange Apes by Lauren Utan

ZANE: I heard they taught monkeys to fly.

KELLY: You're kidding!

ZANE: Nope. They're called hot-air baboons!

What do you get when King Kong walks through your vegetable garden?

Squash.

A sloth was standing in the middle of a busy street when a police officer came by. The sloth asked, "Can you tell me how to get to the hospital?"

The officer answered, "Sure. Keep standing where you are."

What kind of key opens a banana?
A monkey.

What do you call a monkey that eats a lot of potato chips?
A chipmunk.

Why did the gorilla like the banana?
Because it had appeal.

What did the gorilla call his wife?
His prime-mate.

What do you call an exploding monkey?
A ba-boom.

DANNY: What do you call a gorilla wearing earmuffs?

DOUG: I don't know. What?

DANNY: It doesn't matter. He can't hear you.

Why did the lemur cross the road?
He had to take care of some monkey business.

What did the gorilla eat before dinner?
An ape-etizer.

What is black and white and has sixteen wheels?
A capuchin wearing roller skates.

What side of a monkey has the most fur?
  The outside.

How do monkeys get downstairs?
  They slide down the bananaster.

Knock, knock.

Who's there?

Monkey.

Monkey who?

Monkey won't fit. That's why I knocked!

What do you call a restaurant that throws food in your face?

A monkey business.

What do you call a 500-pound gorilla?

Sir.

TONGUE TWISTERS

So many monkeys smile sneakily.

Shocked chimps chided sleeping sheep.

Are orangutans always orange?

Apes ate green grapes.

Cheeky chimps in trees chase each other.

The more Maura mimes monkeys, the less
    Lester likes lemurs.

Galloping Giggles

A man rode his horse to town on Friday.
The next day, he rode back on Friday.
How is this possible?

The horse's name was Friday.

Why did the pony go to the doctor?
Because it was a little horse.

What is a horse's favorite salad dressing?
Ranch.

How is a horse like a wedding?
They both need a groom.

FARMER: Are you a horse? Yea or nay?
HORSE: Neighhhh!
FARMER: Then I guess you're not a horse!

What did the horse say when it tripped?
"Oh no! I can't giddyup!"

What is a horse's favorite sport?
Stable tennis.

Knock, knock.
Who's there?
Yee.
Yee who?
What are you? A cowboy?

How many legs does a horse have if you call its tail a leg?

Four. Calling its tail a leg doesn't make it one!

When does a horse talk?

Whinny wants to.

What do you call a clumsy horse?

A Collides-dale.

A man in a movie theater noticed what looked like a horse sitting next to him. "Are you a horse?" asked the man, surprised.

"Yes."

"What are you doing at the movies?"

The horse replied, "Well, I liked the book."

Why do people ride horses?

Because they're too heavy to carry.

Who do horses like to visit?
  Their neigh-bors.

What does it mean when you find a horseshoe?
  Some poor horse is walking around in just his socks.

CALLI: What's the difference between a horse and a duck?

SALLY: I don't know. What?

CALLI: One goes quick, and the other goes quack!

How does a horse vote?
   He says "yea" or "neigh."

Why did the horse eat with his mouth open?
   It had bad stable manners.

AGRICULTURE STUDENT: How long should a horse's legs be?

AGRICULTURE TEACHER: Long enough to reach the ground.

How did the pony learn multiplication?
   Using times stables.

TONGUE TWISTERS

Pretty pintos and painted ponies prance around
the paddock.

Hungry horses horde heaps of hay.

The Appaloosa ate eight apples.

Mighty mustang stallions must impress
mustang mares.

Where do horses go when they're sick?
The horsepital.

Why did the roller-skating horse get hurt?
She wasn't wearing neighpads (kneepads).

Knock, knock.
Who's there?
Yukon.
Yukon who?
Yukon lead a horse to water, but you can't
    make it drink.

Reptile Romps and Amphibian Antics

What kind of snake keeps its
car the cleanest?
A windshield viper.

Knock, knock.
Who's there?
Iguana.
Iguana who?
Iguana hold your hand.

What is a frog's favorite song?
"Head, Shoulders, Knees, and Toads."

How does a rooster wake up a crocodile?
He says, "Croc-a-doodle-doo!"

What did the bus driver say to the frog?
"Hop on!"

SNAKE #1: Are we venomous?
SNAKE #2: Yes. Why?
SNAKE #1: I just bit my lip!

What did the snake give his wife?
A goodnight hiss.

What is a toad's favorite game?
Croak-et (croquet).

AUDREY: My pet turtle turned two today!

MALCOLM: Cool! Are you going to shellebrate his birthday?

What type of snake builds things?
A boa constructor.

What do iguanas put on their kitchen floors?
Rep-tiles.

How does a snake practice archery?
With a boa and arrow.

Knock, knock.
Who's there?
Alli.
Alli who?
Alligator, that's who.

What do you get when you cross a pig and a frog?

A hamphibian.

What did the frog order for lunch?

French flies and a large croak.

When does a lizard say "quack"?
When he's trying to learn a new language.

What did the turtle say to his friend when he left?
"Turtle-loo!"

Where do funny frogs sit?
On silly pads.

One day while crossing the road, a snail was hit by a turtle. At the hospital, the doctor asked, "How did it happen?"

"I can't remember," said the snail. "It all happened so fast."

What is a snake's favorite river?
The Hississippi.

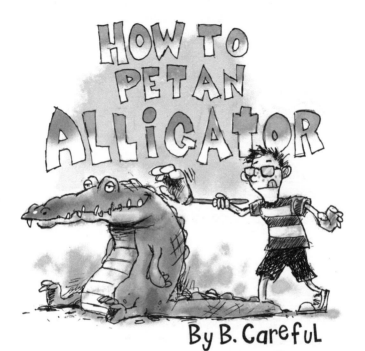

Turtle Legs by Mo Slow

Bug Sandwiches by Liz Ardchow

Frog Chairs by Lily Padd

Big Green Snakes by Anna Conda

How to Pet an Alligator by B. Careful

How Small Are Baby Turtles? by Justine E.

What do you get when you cross a science-fiction film with a toad?
   Star Warts.

What did the mom chameleon say to her nervous kid on the first day of school?
"Don't worry. You'll blend right in!"

MALIK: Is it true that an alligator won't attack you if you're carrying a flashlight?

DAISY: It depends on how fast you're carrying the flashlight!

What was the turtle doing on the highway?
About one mile an hour.

Why did the snake laugh so hard she cried?
Because she thought the joke was hiss-terical.

What goes *dot-dot-croak, dot-dash-croak?*
Morse toad.

What's the difference between a dog and a crocodile?

One's bark is worse than his bite, and one's bite is worse than his bark.

Knock, knock.
Who's there?
Viper.
Viper who?
Please viper runny nose.

What do you get when you cross a snake and a fruit-filled dessert?

A pie-thon.

What do you call an alligator who is wearing a vest?

An investigator.

What kind of phone does a turtle use?
A shell phone.

Two frogs were sitting on a lily pad, eating lunch. One said to the other, "Time sure is fun when you're having flies."

Why did the salamander feel lonely?
Because he was newt to the area.

What do you call a woman with a frog on her head?
Lily.

ERIC: Go look in the cage over there. You'll see a ten-foot snake.

DERYCK: Don't try to kid me—snakes don't have feet!

What do you get if you cross a toad and a dog?
A croaker spaniel.

What powerful reptile can you find in the Emerald City?
The Lizard of Oz.

What kind of pole is short and floppy?
A tadpole.

JACK: Can you please measure that snake over there?

PIPER: How would you like me to measure it?

JACK: In inches. They don't have any feet!

What is worse than one crocodile coming to dinner?

Two crocodiles coming to dinner.

FROG: So, doctor, what is the diagnosis?
DOCTOR: I'm afraid you're going to need a hop-eration.

What is a turtle's favorite thing to wear in winter?

A turtleneck.

What did the lizard say to the other lizard?
"Iguana be your friend!"

What is a snake's favorite kind of shoe?
Ssssssssneakers.

Knock, knock.
Who's there?
Dragon.
Dragon who?
You're dragon your feet again.

What is green and red?
A very mad frog.

What did the turtle say to his surfing turtle friend?
"You're turtally awesome."

What does a frog wear on Saint Patrick's Day?

Nothing!

How can you revive a snake that looks dead?

With mouse-to-mouth resuscitation.

LULA: What kind of shoes do frogs wear?

NADIA: I don't know. What kind?

LULA: Open-toad sandals.

What do snakes use to cut paper?

Scissssors.

What kind of bull doesn't have horns?

A bullfrog.

How did the turtle get off his back?

He rocked and rolled.

What do you call a crocodile with a GPS system?
A navi-gator.

What kind of snake is good at math?
An adder.

Why are frogs so happy?
Because they eat what bugs them.

What did the snake say to his little sister?
"Stop being such a rattle-tail!"

What did the frog dress up as on Halloween?
A prince.

What kind of amphibian loves to tell jokes?
A silly-mander.

What do you get when you cross kangaroos with geckos?

Leaping lizards!

What kind of turtles are green and easy to see?

Green sea turtles.

What happened when the frog broke down on the highway?

He got toad away.

What is a crocodile's favorite drink?

Gator-ade.

Two frogs are watching a play at the theater.
FROG #1: What do you think of this show?
FROG #2: I think it is toad-ally awesome!

Knock, knock.
Who's there?
Toad.
Toad who?
Toad you I knew a good knock-knock joke.

If you crossed a snake with a robin, what kind of bird would you get?
  A swallow.

If lizards had their own country, what would it be called?
  Gecko-slovakia.

ELLIE: What do you get when you cross a snake and a frog?
SPENCER: I don't know. What?
ELLIE: A jump rope!

Tiny turtles tried on tutus.
On Sunday, several sneaky
    salamanders escaped.
Don't trouble timid turtles.
Some skinks slither, some lizards slink.
Green geckos gallop gracefully.
Twenty-two tired toads tied twine.
Four fat frogs flying past fast.
Three tree-frog families float freely for fun.
Slithering silver snakes sneakily snuck away.
Some legless lizards, like skinks, slither skillfully
    like snakes.

Wacky Wildlife

What is a rabbit's favorite candy?
Lollihops.

What game do mice like to play?
Hide-and-squeak.

RONAN: What do you call a deer with no eyes?
AVERY: I have no-eye deer.
RONAN: What do you call a deer with no eyes
    and no legs?
AVERY: Still no-eye deer.

What animal likes letters?
  An alphabat.

Knock, knock.
Who's there?
Mice.
Mice who?
Mice to meet you.

What do you get if you cross a rabbit with fleas?
  A bugs bunny.

How do you
stop a skunk
from smelling?
  *You hold
  its nose.*

Why did the squirrel take so long to eat the walnut?

It was one tough nut to crack.

A raccoon was walking through the woods and came to a river. She looked upstream and downstream in search of a bridge, but she could not find one. Seeing another raccoon on the opposite bank, she called, "Do you know how to get to the other side?"

"You *are* on the other side!" the raccoon called back.

EVIE: How do you catch a unique rabbit?

STEVIE: How?

EVIE: Unique up on it! How do you catch a tame rabbit?

STEVIE: I don't know.

EVIE: The tame way.

What mouse was a Roman emperor?
Julius Cheeser.

Where do rabbits go after their wedding?
On their bunnymoon.

Why did the porcupine win the game?
He had the most points.

What do you call a lost wolf?
A where-wolf.

RAMI: Where did the squirrel store his food?

WYATT: I don't know. Where?

RAMI: In his pan-tree!

Knock, knock.

Who's there?

Bat.

Bat who?

I'll bat you can't guess.

How do you know carrots are good for your eyes?

> *You never see rabbits wearing glasses, do you?*

What do you get when you cross Bambi with a ghost?

> *Bamboo.*

Why did Emma bring her skunk to school?
For show-and-smell.

How can you tell old rabbits from young rabbits?
Look for the gray hares.

LENNY: What do you get when you cross a porcupine and a turtle?
JENNY: I don't know. What?
LENNY: A slowpoke.

What did one wolf say to another?
"Let's go catch some fast food."

How do rabbits travel?
By hareplane.

A duck, a deer, and a skunk went out to dinner. When the waiter brought the check, the deer said he didn't have a buck, and the skunk said he didn't have a scent. So they put it on the duck's bill!

What did the beaver say to the tree?
"It was nice gnawing (knowing) you."

Knock, knock.
Who's there?
Moose.
Moose who?
Moose you be so nosy?

Who did the deer invite to his birthday party?
His nearest and deer-est friends.

What is a skunk's favorite sandwich?
Peanut butter and smelly.

What do rabbits use to measure diamonds?
Carrots (carats).

What did the wolf say when someone stepped on his foot?
"Aoooowwwwww!"

What is small, furry, and brilliant at sword fights?
A mouseketeer.

DOCTOR: What brings you to my office today?

SQUIRREL: I just realized that I am what I
    eat. Nuts!

What do you call a rabbit who is angry in the
summertime?
    A hot cross bunny.

How many skunks does it take to make a
big stink?
    A phew.

Hickory, dickory, dock.
Two mice ran up the clock.
The clock struck one,
And the other one got away.

Where do bunnies live?
    In a rabbitat.

Why did the wolf cross the road?
He was chasing the chicken!

Where do hamsters come from?
Hamsterdam.

Knock, knock.
Who's there?
Beaver E.
Beaver E. who?
Beaver E. quiet and nobody will hear us.

MAYA: Where are you taking that skunk?
AARON: To the gym.
MAYA: What about the smell?
AARON: Oh, he'll get used to it.

What kind of party do mice throw when they move into a new home?
A mouse-warming party.

What is a female deer's favorite ice-cream flavor?
Cookie doe.

What did the porcupine say to the cactus?
"Are you my mother?"

What did the judge say when the skunk walked into the courtroom?

"Odor in the court!"

*One day a bat left to get food and returned
with a huge bump on his head.*

BAT #1: What happened?

BAT #2: You see that tree over there?

BAT #1: Yes.

BAT #2: Well, I didn't.

What happened when five hundred hares got
loose on Main Street?

The police had to comb the area.

What do you call a flying skunk?

A smelly-copter.

Knock, knock.

Who's there?

Weasel.

Weasel who?

Weasel while you work.

What is a bunny's favorite kind of music?
   Hip hop.

How much money does a skunk have?
   One scent.

How do you catch a squirrel?
   Climb a tree and act like a nut.

Knock, knock.
Who's there?
Rabbit.
Rabbit who?
Please rabbit up for me—it's a present for
   my mom.

Rapid rabbits ran rampant.

Big bats bite bitter berries.

Waddling wild ducks dawdle.

Don't double-dare daring deer!

Squirrel squished squash.

Ravenous rabbits roasted radishes.

Daring deer don't dawdle.

The shy, sleepy groundhog was shocked to
see his shadow.

Daffy Dinos

What do you get if you give a dinosaur
a pogo stick?
   Big holes in your driveway.

What is a butcher's favorite dinosaur?
The steak-osaurus.

What was *T. rex*'s favorite number?
Eight (ate).

DARYL: Why did the triceratops cross the road?
ROSA: I thought the chicken crossed the road.
DARYL: Well, why did the chicken cross the road?
ROSA: I don't know. Why?
DARYL: To get away from the triceratops!

Why do museums have old dinosaur bones?
They can't afford new ones.

What happened when the dinosaur took the train home?
His mom made him bring it back.

What do you call a million-year-old dinosaur?
  A fossil.

What is a dinosaur when it gets out of a bath?
  Ex-stinked.

What type of tool does a prehistoric reptile carpenter use?

A dino-saw.

SHIVANI: Why was the stegosaurus afraid to go to the library?

JAMES: I don't know. Why?

SHIVANI: Because her books were millions of years overdue!

What do you call it when two dinosaurs crash into each other?

A *Tyrannosaurus wreck.*

What do you call a dinosaur with an extensive vocabulary?

A *thesaurus.*

Knock, knock.

Who's there?

T. rex.

T. rex who?

There's a *T. rex* at your door and you want to know its name?!

What did the dinosaur call her shirt-making business?

Try Sarah's Tops.

What do you call a sleeping dinosaur?
Dino-snorus.

What do you ask a thirsty dinosaur?
"Tea, Rex?"

What is a dinosaur's favorite lunch?
Macaroni and trees.

When can three brontosauruses hide under a small umbrella and not get wet?
When it's not raining!

What was the scariest prehistoric animal?
The terror-dactyl.

What's the best way to talk to a velociraptor?
Long distance.

How do archeologists find dinosaur princesses?

They follow the dinosaur prints (prince).

What did the triceratops sit on?

Its tricerabottom.

What do you get if you cross a dinosaur and a football player?

A quarterback no one can tackle.

What do you call a polite dinosaur?

A *Please-iosaur.*

Why did carnivorous dinosaurs eat their meat raw?

Because they didn't know how to barbecue.

Knock, knock.
Who's there?
Dinosaur.
Dinosaur who?
Dinosaurs don't go who. They go ROAR!

WIFE: Dear, did the dinosaur take a bath?
HUSBAND: Why, is there one missing?

What do you call an injured dinosaur?
  Dino-sore.

What kind of dinosaur wakes up early?
  A crackodon (crack o' dawn).

HARPER: I don't know what to do. I lost my
  pet iguanodon!
LUKE: Why don't you put an ad in the paper?
HARPER: What good would that do? He can't read!

TEACHER: Libby, can you name ten dinosaurs in ten seconds?

LIBBY: Sure. Eight iguanodons and two stegosauruses.

What do you call a *Tyrannosaurus rex* when he wears a cowboy hat and boots?

Tyrannosaurus tex.

ANNIE: What do you call a nearsighted dinosaur?

MILO: I don't know. What?

ANNIE: Doyathinkhesaurus?

MILO: Well then, what do you call his dog?

ANNIE: I don't know. What?

MILO: Doyouthinkhesaurus Rex.

What do you get if you cross a triceratops with a kangaroo?

A tricera-hops.

The *T. rex* tripped twice.

Dr. Docker determinedly digs for dinosaur fossils.

A pterodactyl trio perched precariously on treetops.

Stanley, I'm certain that stegosaurus saw us.

Dozing, snoring dinosaurs do snooze snuggly.

Brave brontosaurus babies break branches.

Sillies on Safari

What do you get when two giraffes collide?
A giraffic jam.

How do you talk to an elephant that's far away?
Use an elephone.

How can you tell a water buffalo from a mouse?
*Try to pick it up. If you can't, it's a
water buffalo.*

How does a lion greet the other animals
in the savannah?

"Pleased to eat you!"

A doctor looks into a patient's ear.

DOCTOR: I think I see a whole herd of elephants
in there!

PATIENT: Herd of elephants?

DOCTOR: Of course I've heard of elephants.
Haven't you?

What do you get when you cross a kangaroo
with an elephant?

Great big holes all over Australia.

Knock, knock.

Who's there?

Rhino.

Rhino who?

Rhino every knock-knock joke there is.

MAN: I rode a hippo to work yesterday.

WOMAN: Surely you can't be serious!

MAN: I am serious, and please don't call me Shirley.

What's as big as an elephant but weighs nothing?

An elephant's shadow.

What state do lions like best?

Maine (mane).

Knock, knock.

Who's there?

Lionel.

Lionel who?

Lionel bite you if you put your head in its mouth.

Why don't cheetahs ever take baths?
Because they don't want to be spotless.

What kind of illness can a zebra get?
Stripe throat.

What wears glass slippers and weighs ten thousand pounds?

Cinderellephant.

If the alphabet goes from *A* to *Z*, what goes from *Z* to *A*?

A zebra.

What is a vampire's favorite animal?

A giraffe.

"I found the escaped leopard," the park ranger reported by two-way radio. "It's about one-hundred feet away from me. What should I do now?"

"Tranquilize it on the spot," came the reply.

"Which spot?" responded the ranger.

What do you call a male hippopotamus?

hippopota-mister.

GIRAFFE #1: I'm going to hike up that mountain. Would you like to come?

GIRAFFE #2: No, thank you. I'm afraid of heights.

GIRAFFE #1: How are you afraid of heights? You're a giraffe!

What did the rhino say to Napoleon Bonaparte?
Nothing. Rhinos don't speak French.

What would you do if an elephant sat in front of you in a movie theater?

Miss most of the film.

What do you call a hippo in a phone booth?

Stuck.

What side of a cheetah has the most spots?
The outside.

Why do giraffes have long necks?
Because their feet smell!

ELEPHANT #1: Did you hear about the race
between the two giraffes?
ELEPHANT #2: I heard it was neck and neck!

How does a lion paddle a canoe?
He uses his roar.

What is a leopard's favorite day?
Chewsday.

What are old bowling balls used as?
Marbles for elephants.

Where can you win the world's tallest animal?
At a gi-raffle.

A lion was playing checkers with a cheetah.
The cheetah skipped across the board and
got all the checkers in one move. "You're a
cheetah!" said the lion. "You're lion!" said
the cheetah.

What did the elephant say when he saw
something gross?
"That is grotusk!"

Why is a leopard bad at hiding?
Because it's always spotted.

What is gray but can turn red?
An embarrassed rhinoceros.

HANNAH: What do you call an elephant that never takes a bath?

FELIX: I don't know. What?

HANNAH: A smellyphant.

What do you get when you cross a cheetah and a sheep?

A polka-dotted sweater.

Knock, knock.

Who's there?

Hippo.

Hippo who?

Hippo birthday to you!

When does a giraffe have eight legs?
  When there are two giraffes.

Why are elephants so wrinkled?
  Well, did you ever try to iron one?

Knock, knock.

Who's there?

Lion.

Lion who?

You're lion down on the job again.

HOW **BIG** Are Hippos?
BY Hugh Mongus

Large Mammals by L. E. Fant
Chased by a Cheetah by Ronan Fast
How Big Are Hippos? by Hugh Mongus
Animals with Long Necks by G. Raffe
The Lion Pride by King Adda Jungle

Knock, knock.
Who's there?
Safari.
Safari who?
Safari so good!

What do you call a rhino at the North Pole?
Lost.

What time is it when an elephant sits on your fence?

Time to fix the fence.

Why did the giraffe sit on the marshmallow?

So she wouldn't fall into the hot chocolate.

What do you get if you cross a zebra with an ape man?

Tarzan stripes.

Why do elephants have trunks?

They'd look pretty silly with glove compartments.

What's the best thing to do if an elephant sneezes?

Get out of its way!

Knock, knock.

Who's there?

Giraffe.

Giraffe who?

Giraffe anything to eat? I'm hungry!

What do you need to know if you want to be a lion tamer?

More than the lion.

Where do Italian elephants live?

Tusk-any.

Why don't elephants and zebras like playing cards in the jungle?

There are too many cheetahs.

What is black and white and blue?

A zebra with a cold.

Why did the rhino cross the road?
    *He thought, "If the chicken can do it, so
    can I!"*

What does a hippo get if he stops shaving?
    A hippopata-mustache.

Why is a giraffe a bad dinner guest?
    It eats, leaves.

What do elephants do for laughs?
They tell people jokes.

Why did the old hippo go to the hospital?
He needed a hippoperation.

JOE: What do you call a truck full of bison?

DANNY: I have no clue.

JOE: A buffa-load!

Pretend you are in Africa and a cheetah is chasing you. What do you do?

Stop pretending!

What is the difference between an African rhino and an Indian rhino?

About three thousand miles.

TEACHER: Naomi, what is your favorite animal?

NAOMI: A hippopotamus.

TEACHER: Wonderful. Now please spell it.

NAOMI: Oh, I've changed my mind. My favorite animal is a lion.

What is the difference between an injured lion and a cloud?

One pours with rain, and the other roars with pain!

What is tall and smells good?

A giraffodil.

How do you know when a rhino is about to charge?

He asks, "Will that be all, sir?"

Why is an elephant big, gray, and lumpy?

Because if it were small, white, and smooth, it would be a mint.

Why can't you play football with rhinos?

Because they're too hard to tackle.

What is black and white and black and white
and black and white?
A zebra in a revolving door.

What did the cashier say when she saw the
giraffe standing in line?
"Necks!"

Why don't giraffes ever learn how to swim? *Because it's easier just to walk on the bottom of the pool.*

SHERMAN: Do you know what the biggest ant in the world is?

MASON: No. What is it?

SHERMAN: An elephant!

TONGUE TWISTERS

Lazing lions gaze at gazelles.
Giraffes give gazelles grapes.

Elephants led the elaborate antics.
Rare rhinos rolled real red wagons.
Hilly Hippo hollered hello.
Chilly cheetahs chow on chewy cherries.
Hiccupping hippos.
Intelligent elephants are excellent smellers.
White rhinos write witty rhymes.

Beary Funny

What is a polar bear's favorite
ride at the amusement park?
The polar coaster.

What do you call a bear with no fur?
   A bare bear.

Why do pandas like old movies?
   Because they're in black and white.

What do you get when you cross a bear
with a rain cloud?
   A drizzly bear.

Knock, knock.
Who's there?
Grrr.
Grrr who?
Are you a bear or an owl?

Where do you find polar bears?
   It depends on where you lost them.

What do you call bears without ears?
   B's.

BRAD: Why do bears paint their faces yellow?

TAKARA: I don't know. Why?

BRAD: So they can hide in banana trees.

TAKARA: Impossible! I've never seen a bear in a banana tree.

BRAD: See? It works!

Where do polar bears vote?
The North Poll.

Knock, knock.
Who's there?
Aurora.
Aurora who?
Aurora's just come from that big polar bear.

Why do pandas have fur coats?
Because they don't look as good in denim jackets.

How does a bear stop a movie?
She presses the "paws" button.

What do polar bears do on the computer?
They surf the Winternet.

Why didn't the cub leave his mommy?
He couldn't bear it!

What wild animal might you find in a
dentist's office?
A molar bear.

RON: What kind of sandwiches do bears like?

JOHN: I don't know. What kind?

RON: Growled-cheese sandwiches!

Why was the polar bear upset with her test grades?

They were all twenty below zero.

What do you get when you cross a skunk with a bear?

Winnie the P-U.

What do Asian bears eat for breakfast?

Panda-cakes.

What do you call a bear with no teeth?

A gummy bear.

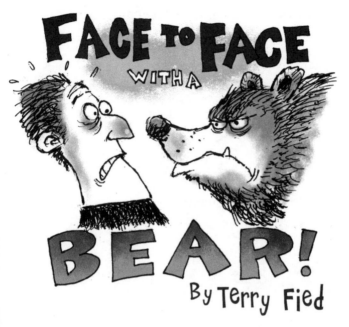

FACE TO FACE WITH A BEAR!
By Terry Fied

Black and White by Ima Panda
What Bears Do Best by Clem Trees
Face to Face with a Bear by Terry Fied
Where Polar Bears Play by Indy Snow
I Hear a Growling Sound by Chris Lee Bear

How does a polar bear build its house?
Igloos it together.

What kind of bad dreams do grizzly
bears have?
Bitemares.

What do polar bears eat for lunch?
Ice berg-ers.

TRINITY: What do you get when you cross a bear and a skunk?

KRISTY: I don't know. What?

TRINITY: I don't know either, but it can easily get a seat on the bus!

What goes black, white, black, white, black, white?
A panda rolling down a hill.

Why did the bear get so scared?
He looked in the mirror.

Where does a polar bear keep all his money?
In a snowbank.

Knock, knock.
Who's there?
Icy.
Icy who?
Icy a big polar bear.

What do you call a bear with no socks?
   Bear foot (barefoot).

What happened to the panda that fell out of the tree?
   He got a bambooboo.

TONGUE TWISTERS

Brown bears barely notice nosy neighbors.

Grumpy grizzlies growl gruffly.

Black bears baked braided bread.

A big black bear sat on a big black bug.

"Please!" pandas pleaded.

All the Rest

What animal
hates cold feet?
*A mother
kangaroo.*

Knock, knock.
Who's there?
Panther.
Panther who?
Panther what I wear on my legth.

LUCY: Excuse me. Where are the otters?
ZOO EMPLOYEE: They're on the otter side
of the zoo.

What is a camel's
favorite nursery
rhyme?
*Humpty
Dumpty.*

SADIE: Where did the ferret go when he lost his tail?

DESMOND: I don't know. Where?

SADIE: To the retail store.

Knock, knock.
Who's there?
Mammoth.
Mammoth who?
Mammoth is sthuck 'cause I'th been eatin' peanut buther.

One day at the zoo, the kangaroo got out. So the zookeeper made the fence higher. The kangaroo got out again, so the zookeeper made the fence even higher. This went on until the fence was 15 feet high. Finally, the kangaroo said to the giraffe, who lived on the other side of the fence, "I wish the zookeeper would stop wasting his money on the fence and start shutting the door!"

What is the fiercest flower in the garden?
 A tiger lily.

What did the elk say to his loud roommate?
 "Moose you be so noisy?"

What is a llama's favorite food?
 Llama beans.

What do you get when you cross peanut butter
with a buffalo?
 *You either get peanut butter that roams the
 range or a buffalo that sticks to the roof of
 your mouth.*

What did the otter say to his sister, who just
pulled a prank on him?
 "This is otterly ridiculous."

Knock, knock.

Who's there?

Aardvark.

Aardvark who?

Aardvark a hundred miles for you.

What did the otter say to the superstar?
"Can I have your otter-graph?"

What do you call a camel that has no humps?
Humphrey (Hump-free).

Why doesn't the mother kangaroo like
rainy days?
Because her children have to play inside.

Knock, knock.
Who's there?
Ocelot.
Ocelot who?
You ocelot of questions, don't you?

What kind of buffalo can jump higher
than a building?
Any buffalo because buildings can't jump!

Knock, knock.
Who's there?
Llama.
Llama who?
"Llama Yankee Doodle Dandy."

When do kangaroos celebrate their birthdays?
During leap year.

What is a mole's favorite book?
The digtionary.

Knock, knock.
Who's there?
Kanga.
Kanga who?
Kangaroo, silly!

What is a llama's favorite drink?
Llama-nade.

A yak told a joke to an egg.
EGG: That was so funny! Uh-oh.
YAK: What's wrong?
EGG: You cracked me up!

BOOKS NEVER WRITTEN

Hippity Hoppety by Kendra Roo

Journey Across the Sahara by Rhoda Camel

Look in That Tree by Kala Bear

I Look Like an Elk by Carrie Bou

I Like Stripes by Ty Gerr

What is a tiger's favorite
Christmas carol?
"Jungle Bells."

What do zoo animals wear when they go
swimming?
Zoo-kinis.

Knock, knock.
Who's there?
Alpaca.
Alpaca who?
Alpaca the trunk, you pack-a the suitcase.

Yellow yaks wear speckled slacks.

Sue's new gnu knew shoes!

Many moose munch much mush.

Kevin cared for cave critters.

Yawning yaks sat stacking black hats.

The other otter uttered eighty idioms.

If goose goes to geese, do two moose
  make meese?

Twelve tigers twirled twelve twigs.

Knock, knock.
Who's there?
Bison.
Bison who?
Bison new shoes. Those are worn out!

What should you
do if you find a yak
in your bed?
   Sleep on the sofa.